THEODORE

FRANK KEATING

PAINTINGS BY
MIKE WIMMER

A PAULA WISEMAN BOOK
Simon & Schuster Books for Young Readers
New York London Toronto Sydney

To Catie, Hadley, and Will, the first in a fun line of grandchildren. May they be patriots and hardy lovers of the legacy of Theodore Roosevelt.
—F. K.

Dedicated to my family; like it was for Theodore Roosevelt, it is their love and support that has inspired me and nurtured my God-given abilities to help me achieve all that I am capable of. "Greatness is destined to be carved in stone."
—M. W.

Acknowledgments

The author and publisher gratefully acknowledge the assistance of the Theodore Roosevelt Association, the Theodore Roosevelt birthplace in New York City, and Wallace Dailey at the Theodore Roosevelt Collection at Harvard College Library in creating this book.

The illustrator gratefully acknowledges Wallace Dailey of the Theodore Roosevelt Collection at Harvard University, Dr. John A. Gable of the Theodore Roosevelt Association, the staff of the Oyster Bay Roosevelt home, and the staff of the Theodore Roosevelt birthplace in New York City.

SIMON & SCHUSTER BOOKS FOR YOUNG READERS
An imprint of Simon & Schuster Children's Publishing Division
1230 Avenue of the Americas, New York, New York 10020
Text copyright © 2006 by Frank Keating
Illustrations copyright © 2006 by Mike Wimmer
All rights reserved, including the right of reproduction in whole or in part in any form.
SIMON & SCHUSTER BOOKS FOR YOUNG READERS is a trademark of Simon & Schuster, Inc.
Book design by Daniel Roode
The text for this book is set in Regula.
The paintings for this book are rendered in oil on canvas.
Manufactured in the United States of America
2 4 6 8 10 9 7 5 3 1
CIP data for this book is available from the Library of Congress.
ISBN-13: 978-0-689-86532-9
ISBN-10: 0-689-86532-5

All quotations are the words of Theodore Roosevelt.

Selected Bibliography
Auchincloss, Louis. *Theodore Roosevelt.* New York: Times Books, 2002.
Brands, H. W. *T.R., The Last Romantic.* New York: Basic Books, 1997.
Morris, Edmund. *The Rise of Theodore Roosevelt.* New York: Modern Library, 2001.

"No ability, no strength and force, no power of intellect or power of wealth, shall avail us, if we have not the root of right living in us."

Theodore Roosevelt

*M*y mother named me Theodore, but everyone remembers me as Teddy.

I grew up to be big and broad and strong. As a man I led a nation to greatness. Some said that I was born to greatness.

It was not quite that way.

I was not born big or strong.

But I did know what I wanted and worked at it every day. My goal was to do big things.

"The best prize that life offers is the chance to work hard at work worth doing," I believed.

I was born on October 27, 1858, in New York City, the second of four children.

As a child I was frail. My health frequently kept me indoors. There I read and dreamed to the farthest faraways of my imagination.

"I was nervous and timid."

But reading about the people I admired from history, the soldiers of Valley Forge and Morgan's Riflemen, filled me with excitement and hope.

My illness made me more determined. I wanted to be strong, like the heroes of America's past about whom I had read.

"I felt a great admiration for men who were fearless and who could hold their own in the world, and I had a great desire to be like them."

While my friends played, I created a special world in my mind. I was fascinated by all living things.

When I was seven, I wrote about the size and shape of a seal I had seen in a fish market.

I was full of curiosity and wonder at all creatures great and small.

When I was nine, I composed a "Natural History on Insects," in which I described an assortment of ants, spiders, ladybugs, fireflies, beetles, and dragonflies.

My mother and I were great friends.

"I jumped with delight when I found you had heard a mockingbird," I wrote to her. "Get some of its feathers if you can."

When I was ten, I started to keep a diary. Reading was my routine, and studying and thinking were as normal to me as sleeping and eating.

I loved to read. I read biographies, histories, and books on birds and all things that walk or crawl.

"I remembered a book that I had read sometime ago . . . the pages of the book came before my eyes."

Without fail I kept up my studies and carefully observed nature's wonders around me.

By age eleven I had seen many things. I had traveled to
Europe with my family, climbed an eight-thousand-foot
mountain, and taken long walks of up to nineteen miles.
My father was my best friend and hiking partner.
Nothing could keep me from his side.

My mother was proud of the growth of my mind. My
father insisted that I strengthen my body. I worked hard
at both.

I had boundless energy.

My family traveled to Egypt and the Holy Land,
where I catalogued and observed zebras, waders,
ziczacs, kites, vultures, and water buffalo.

There was so much to learn. I wanted to know everything
and understand all that I saw.

By age fifteen I had sailed to Britain, Europe, North Africa, and the Middle East. I had hunted jackals on horseback, climbed the Great Pyramid, and peered into a volcano.

It was fun. "Isn't this bully?" I exclaimed to my brothers and sisters.

Life with my family was great excitement, a glorious mixture of colors and quests, of drama and dreams.

"I have never spent an unhappy day." I made every day count.

I had many heroes, and I read about the people I most admired—people I wanted to become. They were lovers of freedom.

While still in my twenties I wrote books about the westward expansion; the Naval War of 1812; and American heroes, including biographies of Thomas Hart Benton and Gouverneur Morris. I wrote thirty-five books in all, always celebrating "the joy of life and the duty of life."

"I'm happiest with books all around me."

I worked hard.

Before I was thirty, I headed west—to Dakota Territory and the Little Missouri River, the badlands where the crack of a whip and the steady gait of a horse's hooves were constant sounds in a place lonely and forbidding.

"If you are afraid of hard work . . . do not come west," I wrote to a friend.

I was the father of six children.

"I play with the children almost every night." Alice. Ted. Kermit. Ethel. Archie. Quentin. Life at the Roosevelt house was a lively jumble of wrestling, running, shouting, and song. I was always in the thick of all the children's mischief. Later, when I ascended to the nation's highest office, a friend humorously remarked, "The president is about six."

I was a soldier.

When the Spanish-American War came, I was ready. My charge up San Juan Hill, into the flash and fury of screeching shells and screaming combat, brought me fame and the nation's highest award for bravery in combat, the Congressional Medal of Honor.

Those events led me to become president of the United States at forty-two, the youngest man ever to hold that office. But the presidency was only the last event of a lifetime of study and service. Legislator. Civil service commissioner. Police commissioner. Assistant secretary of the Navy. Governor of New York. Vice president of the United States.

Great success came from great effort and big dreams.

My life as a father and as a president taught me to face every challenge with energy and integrity.

"It is character that counts in a nation as in a man."

I was a builder.

I built my life. I also built a family and a better country.

"It is always better to be an original than an imitation."

I constantly strove to be an original.

I followed my heart wherever it led me.

It was a "worthy course"—to be a better person and to make a better land.

That was the life I lived.

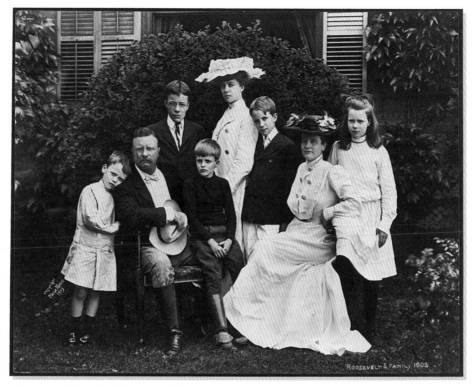

The Roosevelt family (left to right): Quentin, Theodore Roosevelt, Theodore Jr., Archie, Alice, Kermit, Edith Roosevelt, Ethel (Theodore Roosevelt Collection, Harvard College Library)

Theodore Roosevelt (1858"1919) was the twenty-sixth president of the United States. He was born in New York City on October 27, 1858, the second of four children of Theodore and Martha Bulloch Roosevelt. Afflicted with asthma and weak eyes as a young boy, Roosevelt did not let his poor health prevent him from learning and being physically fit. After graduating from Harvard in 1880, he married Alice Hathaway Lee of Chestnut Hill, Massachusetts. She passed away in 1884, leaving one daughter, Alice Lee. Theodore Roosevelt then married Edith Kermit Carow and they had five more children together.

In 1881 Theodore Roosevelt ran for the New York State Legislature and won, holding the office of assemblyman for two terms. In 1884 he purchased a cattle ranch in the badlands of the Dakota Territory, where he lived for two years before returning to New York. There he was defeated in his run for mayor of New York City. Later he organized a group called the Rough Riders, the first U.S. Volunteer Cavalry Regiment, which became nationally known. In 1898 Roosevelt was elected governor of New York. In 1900 Roosevelt accepted the Republican vice-presidential nomination and was elected vice president of the United States. Then, at age forty-two, when fate intervened and President McKinley was assassinated, Roosevelt became president. During his tenure he saw the construction of the Panama Canal and he received the Nobel Peace Prize.

Roosevelt died in his home in Oyster Bay, New York, on January 6, 1919.